The Tao of Living on Purpose

The Tao of Living on Purpose

Judith Morgan
and
Andre de Zanger

HUMANICS NEW AGE

Atlanta, Georgia

The Tao of Living on Purpose
A Humanics Publication

Humanics Trade Publications are an imprint of and published by Humanics Limited, a
division of Humanics Publishing Group, Inc.
Its trademark, consisting of the words Humanics Trade and
the portrayal of a Pegasus, is registered in U.S. Patent and
Trademark Office and in other countries.

Humanics Limited, P.O. Box 7400, Atlanta, GA 30357

Printed in the United States of America

ISBN: 0-89334-284-X
Library of Congress Card Catalog Number 98-85983
Book design by Laura Ross

The Titles of the Chapters

Introduction

The Tao of Living On Purpose is a version of Lao Tzu s poems written with a focus on living a life attuned to one s inner spirit. Lao Tzu, born in 604 B.C., was a keeper of the library in China. He was not a teacher but became known for his wisdom and way of life (the Tao means the Way). Upon his retirement he was asked to put his thoughts into writing. He was wary of doing so because part of his philosophy was to listen to one s inner way rather than to any outside authority. Lao Tzu s emphasis was on Being in the Moment, on Effortless Actions, on Enjoying the Journey rather than the Destination, and on the Importance of Nothingness in order to allow the Somethingness to emerge.

Practicing Your Intuition

These poems can be helpful in gaining new insights into problems or situations facing you. One method of practicing your intuition is to think of a problem, then choose a number from I to 81 at random. Whatever number comes to mind, read that poem and see how it might fit your situation. Another method is to browse through the titles and choose one that speaks to you. As a daily meditation, these poems may help enlighten you Way or Tao in Life.

1. Empty Of Desire

One s true spirit, like the Tao,
Cannot be expressed,
Through words alone.
In the beginning, there were no words,
Yet Heaven and Earth arose,
Then words were created,
And naming gave rise,
To the separate parts of the whole.
What is named,
Are the manifestations of life,
What is nameless,
Is the mysterious source of it all.
Filled with desire,
One may see only the manifestations,
Empty of desire,
A person may experience the source.
Whoever solves this mystery,
Has tapped into that
From whence they arose,
And no longer needs a name,
But if a name be needed,
Wonder could be used,
From wonder to wonder,
Spirit grows.

2. Varying Tones

People finding one thing beautiful,
Think another unbeautiful,
Finding one creation sound,
They judge another unsound.
Yet, creation and destruction,
Difficult and easy, long and short,
High and low, all arise from each other.
Just as something and nothing,
Give birth to one another,
Varying tones make music,
Offer texture to a life,
And nourish the imagination.
A wise person,
Accepts everything as it is,
Letting it come and go,
As something to participate in,
Not to dominate,
To nourish, not possess.
In union with what is,
They give birth freely,
Without claiming authority,
For the spirit is all around,
And within us all.

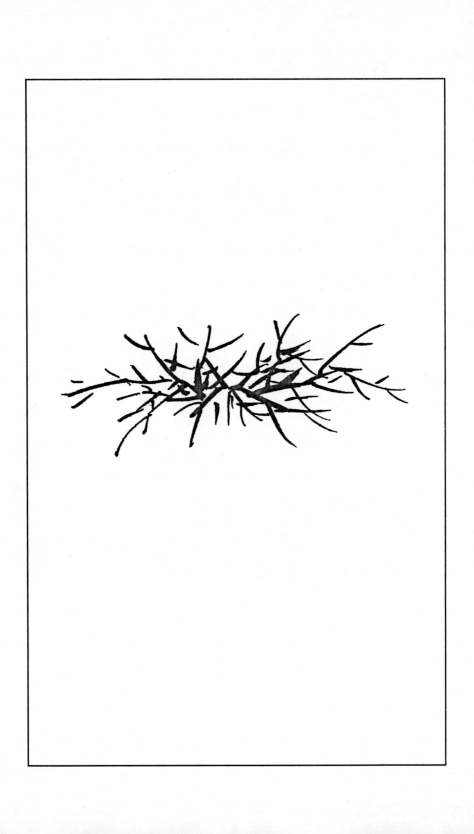

3. Practice Non-Doing

It is better not to praise,
A particular action,
Lest you lose yourself in rivalry,
Not to pile up possessions,
Lest you lose yourself in worry,
Not to excite by boastful display,
Lest you lose yourself in fame.
A person living in tune with themselves,
Will open their heart, calm their will,
And clarify their needs,
So no meddling thoughts can touch them.
When your heart is unconfused,
You can practice non-doing,
And without being forced,
Without struggle or strain,
Fulfillment gains.

4. Running Deep

Imagination is like a never ending well,
Running deep, yet ever present,
Filling up from unknown sources,
Its resourcefulness never fails.
It can be continuously used,
Smoothing sharp edges,
Untangling hard knots,
Softening the sharp sun s glare,
Settling the wind-swept dust.
Filled with unlimited possibilities,
It is both the parent and the child,
Breeding everything, bred by none.

5. Emptiness And Fullness Are One

Not taking sides,
Nature faces the withering of its fruits.
An intuitive person, not taking sides,
Knows that wholeness is like a bellows,
Where the emptiness and fullness are one.
Having faced the living and the dying,
They have no need to study life,
For they do not want to miss,
The joy of living it.

6. To It All Things Flow

One s potential is like a timeless valley,
It lies deep, is sometimes dimly seen,
Yet is always present,
Giving birth to the planted seed.
Because it lies so low,
It cannot fall,
And to it all things flow.
Draw from it all you wish,
The more it is used,
The deeper it grows.

7. Move Out Of The Way

Creativity, like existence,
Beyond the bounds of time,
Lasts forever.
Not self serving,
It is present for all,
And never being an end to itself,
It is endlessly becoming itself.
Move out of the way,
And let it be.

8. Contentment

A person, at their best,
Is like water,
Serving as they go along,
Giving life without striving,
Flowing in all places,
Finding the level
At which they run best.
A person, connected to their spirit,
Will live with a clear and open heart,
Finding contentment,
By simply being themselves,
They intuitively seek their own path,
And in so doing free everyone s way.

9. Doing Without Striving

Keep filling a bowl
And it will spill,
Keep sharpening a blade
And it will dull,
Keep forcing an idea
And block it s way.
Chase after money
And go astray,
Seek other s approval,
And never find your way.
Do enough without striving,
Allow yourself to be.

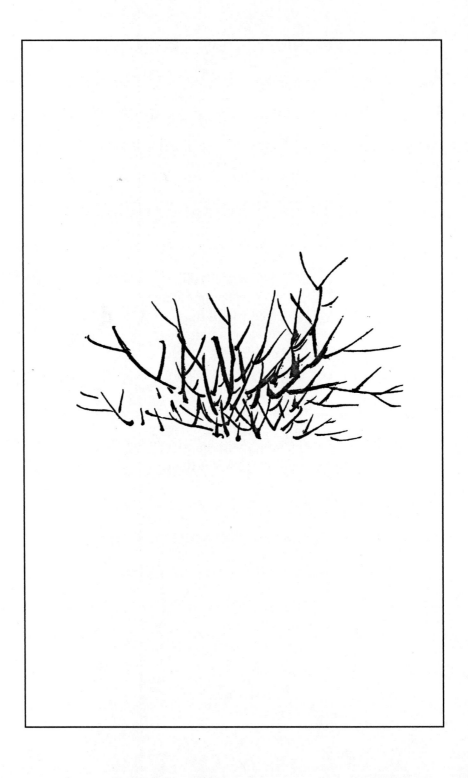

10. Deepening

Hold the door of your being open;
Breathing naturally,
Growing simply,
Staying childlike,
Befriending with no prejudice,
Yet deepening with age.
Allow your active mind to be useful,
Yet not separate you,
From the oneness of all.
Embrace the wisdom of your heart,
And mate with the heavens,
Bear fruit and nourish its growing,
Guiding, without controlling,
Trusting the flow of life.

11. Embracing The Void

Thirty spokes has a wheel,
But it s the hole, the emptiness,
That makes it real.
A bowl is made from clay,
But it s the center, the depth,
That gives it play.
Wood and stone shape a house,
Yet it is the spaces, the openness,
That form a home.
Just as nothing and something,
Combine to become more,
We are helped by the void,
To create the form.

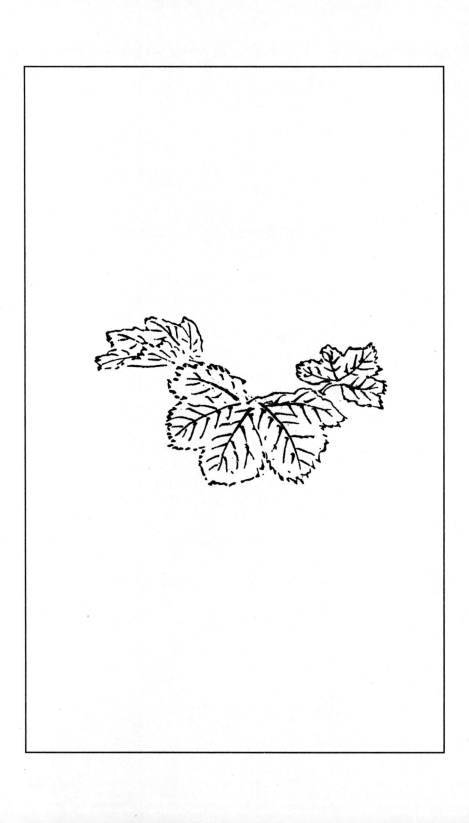

12. The External Pursuit

Looking outside one s self,
Can distract,
Listening outside one s self,
Can confuse.
Just as too many spices
May overwhelm taste,
Too many authorities
May jumble the mind.
The external pursuit
Can rule your life,
And give no joy.
A person, living in fulfillment,
In harmony with their strengths,
Understands that external things
Come and go,
And prefers their within,
To that without.

13. Success And Failure

Success and failure,
Can equally destroy the voice within,
Favor and disfavor,
Can equally stifle one s imagination.
How can success and failure be equal?
Because attending to either,
One will not explore their inner truth.
How can favor and disfavor be equal?
Because being concerned with either,
May leave one in fear of other s judgments.
Success and failure,
Favor and disfavor,
Have no meaning,
To one in touch with their wholeness.
One who knows their inner self,
Understands their oneness with the world,
Attuned to the beauty within,
They celebrate the beauty without,
And are able to care for all.

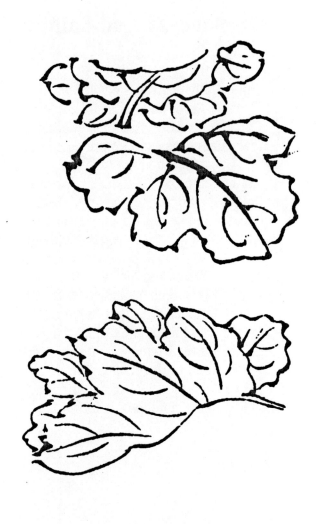

14. Seeking Beyond Seeing

An intuitive person
Seeks beyond seeing,
For the unseen,
Listens beyond hearing,
For the unheard,
Grasps beyond reaching,
For the unreachable,
Goes beyond understanding,
To oneness.
Existence rises and gives light,
Sets and leaves darkness,
Appearing mysteriously,
With no beginning and no end,
It forever sends forth its creations.
One who is aware,
Of this infinite energy,
Is at peace with life.
Moving with the present,
In harmony with each moment,
They live eternally.

15. Flowing Life

Like a stream,
A person s life cannot keeps its course,
If not allowed to flow.
Those who allow themselves to flow,
Have a sense of abundance,
And knowing they need no extra force,
Never tire or strain,
And when in turmoil, they find peace,
By staying still,
Knowing the muddy waters will clear.

16. Quiet Your Mind

Quiet your mind of thoughts,
So your heart shall be at peace,
Being at peace,
Your true path may more easily arise.
Inner wisdom, like all healthy vegetation,
Arises, flourishes,
And then returns,
To the root, to the stillness,
From whence it came.
Through returning to the stillness,
Each living thing,
Fulfills its own destiny.
Awareness of this cycle,
Is to face life with open eyes,
With open eyes,
You will see,
That stillness is both the source,
And the destiny of all living things.
By entering into the stillness,
With an open heart,
You become with all of life.

17. The Light Within

Life is best when a person,
Knows the light is within,
Not so good when a person,
Sees it as outside themselves,
And worst when it is denied.
When a person is on their path,
They talk little,
And when their work is done,
Their journey complete,
They feel at one with the universe,
Peaceful and content,
They say, It happened naturally .

18. Intuitive Wisdom

When people lose sight,
Of the inner way,
Their intuitive wisdom,
Soon decays.
Seeking codes and rules
To obey,
Learning and hypocrisy
Are displayed.
Leaders and followers arise,
And creativity slowly dies.

19. Outward Forms

Letting go of rigid learning,
People would be happier,
Being happier,
Playfulness and imagination
Would take hold.
Giving up social rules and duties,
People would rediscover
Their natural compassion,
Being kinder,
Spontaneity and inspiration
Would flow.
Getting rid of excessive profits,
People would have no thieves to fear,
And being unafraid
Freedom would take charge.
These outward forms of life have failed,
Therefore, set yourself free,
Find your own inner wisdom,
Realize your true nature,
And do as you would like to be.

20. Endless Possibilities

Those who follow their inner spirit,
Live with endless possibilities,
And often give up formal learning
To find their own way.
With no need to distinguish
Between success and failure,
They find less absolutes,
And tend not to follow others.
They are like newborn infants,
Seemingly doing nothing, playing,
And sometimes left out.
The average person
Appears so confident and clear,
Succeeding, meeting goals,
And belonging easily among their peers.
While those who live their inner way
Are sometimes like the sea,
Seemingly drifting nowhere
Yet with endless possibilities,
Like a well-loved infant,
Energized by curiosity,
And amazed at the world.

21. The Elusive Origin

Being one with life,
Accept its wholeness,
With no need to understand,
Its intangible source,
Or the elusive origin,
Of its force.
The source may appear,
Dark and empty,
Yet is also radiant,
May appear far away,
Yet is within every moment.
Look inside,
And feel this abundant source,
Filled with infinite potential.
What more need you know,
Than this?

22. Emptying To Be Full

The wholeness of life is such that,
By yielding you can overcome,
By bending you can straighten,
By emptying you can be full,
By dying you can be reborn,
By having little you can gain,
And by having much,
You can be confused.
Aware of this, a creative person,
Embraces wholeness,
And without displaying themselves
They shine,
Without proclaiming themselves,
They are trusted
By not knowing themselves
They begin to truly be themselves,
And by not competing
They only succeed.
Finding peace and competence,
They have the simple rewards
Which other s may desire.
Yield and you need not break,
Empty and you may fill,
Let go and find your own.

23. The Natural Way

Nature does not insist,
That things last forever,
High winds may last
For part of a morning,
Heavy rain for half a day.
If nature does not insist,
Why should you?
Like the forces of nature,
Inspiration is natural too.
It may flow for part of a day,
Hibernate for half a year,
Or illuminate a night.
Open yourself to it,
And feel well used,
Feel at home,
Feel welcome.
Honor the natural way,
And it will honor you.

24. Keeping Balanced

A person who is intuitive,
Does not grasp for the top,
As they know they may lose their balance.
Nor do they run for the goal,
As they know they may lose
The delight of the journey.
Following their inner way,
Keeps them in the light,
So they have no need of boasting,
And feeling connected
To themselves and others,
They have no need of winning.
For these outer things they know,
Do not bring happiness,
And guided by their joy,
They will not be swayed.

25. Expanding Limits

As one is living a creative life,
It is as if a presence existed,
Changeless, yet moving,
Formless, yet complete,
Mateless, yet from its womb,
All things are born.
A presence from which,
All come and all go,
The heart and home of all.
Touching this presence,
Gives a fullness to life,
Widening into space,
Expanding limits,
Completing the circle,
One is made whole.

26. Transforming Chaos

Gravity is at the center,
Of all things,
Speed, time and light all obey.
It conserves and maintains,
Yet stillness is at its core.
A creative person,
Centers themselves,
Staying in balance,
No matter how fast the day.
There is a call for action,
Opportunity awaits,
Yet the master within,
Keeps a calm head,
Sets a pace rooted in gravity,
In stillness,
Transforming chaos into grace.

27. Teacher- Student

A person seeking their purpose
Wanders about,
Trusting their intuition,
Setting no goals,
Using what is not.
Keeping an open mind,
They are good at seeing
That nothing is lost.
Assisting all, abandoning none,
They see themselves in all others,
And all others in themselves.
They know that to guide someone else
They first need to find their own way.
When the teacher becomes the student,
The student is the teacher
And neither loses the road,
For they will both embody the light.

28. Seeing The Beauty

One who has both the strength of a man,
And the gentleness of a woman,
Is open to the world.
One who loves the light,
But also, loves the darkness,
Is whole,
And being whole,
Is abundantly resourceful,
One who knows they are honorable,
And yet is humble,
Accepts themselves,
And, like a child,
Is forever seeing the beauty,
In the Uncarved Block,
In the simplicity,
From which all is formed.

29. Spontaneity

Spontaneity cannot be ruled,
Or ordered about,
Those who attempt to control it,
Never succeed.
Imagination is like a sacred vessel,
Fragile, easily marred,
And, when grasped too firm, it is gone.
There is a time for moving ahead,
And a time for staying behind,
There is a time for safety,
And a time for taking risks,
There is a time for being strong,
And a time for being gentle,
There is a time to gather to one s self,
And a time for letting go.
Those who fulfill their own calling,
Are attuned to these timings,
Allowing things to go their own way,
They stay at the center of their being.

30. The Natural Way

One who would guide others
In finding themselves,
Will warn against the use of force,
As it often drains strength away.
And they know that using too much energy
In the search,
Will leave one dry and decayed.
A good guide will encourage others to seek,
But also to rest and look within.
They will value the inner voice,
And tell others,
To listen to their own music.
They help others
To put aside fame or fortune,
And encourage them
To do what they must do,
Because it is their natural way,
Arising from an inner calling.
Being is not something to conquer or force,
Follow the way of life
And allow yourself to be.

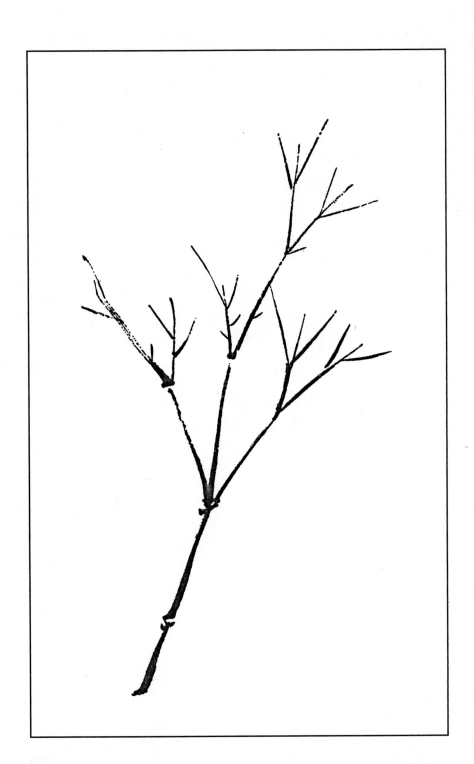

31. Diversity

Weapons create violence,
Force creates fear.
One who is fulfilling their life,
Does not use their energy this way.
Peace and quiet are in their heart,
And victory no cause for joy.
If you rejoice in force,
Then you delight in killing,
If you rejoice in diversity,
Then you delight in living.

32. As Receptive As The Earth

A creative life, like existence,
Is forever,
And needs no definition.
Only when the whole is separated,
Do the parts get named,
And instructions given.
When one adheres to the wholeness of life,
They are in harmony with the universe,
And their inner talents naturally bloom.
Having no need of instructions,
Life is as spontaneous as the rain,
As broad-minded as the clouds,
And as receptive as the earth.
A creative life, like existence,
Is available to all,
Ruled by none,
And is as natural,
As a river flowing to the sea.

33. Wise Strength

Knowledge helps us to understand,
What is outside of ourselves,
While wisdom, arising from our center,
Helps us to love.
Mastery of others requires force,
Mastery of self requires strength.
Ambition can lead us astray,
While contentment is knowing we have enough.
Wisdom, strength, and contentment,
Are like the marrow in our bone,
Loving, supporting and nourishing,
The structure that we are.

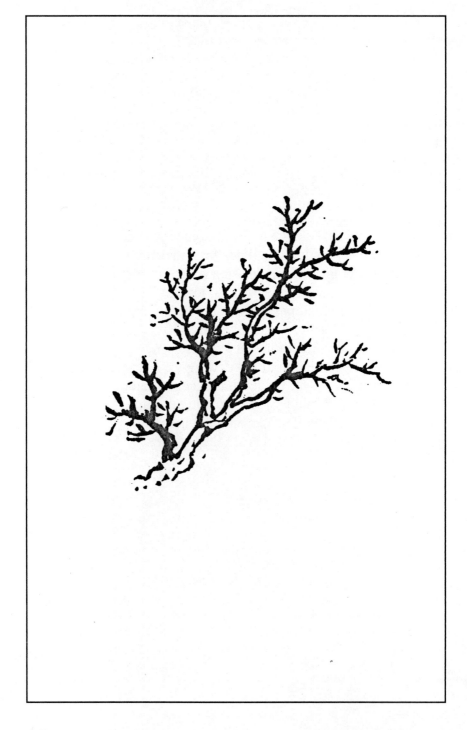

34. Abundance

Abundance,
Like a bountiful host,
Lets everyone attend.
Making no distinctions,
It silently nourishes,
With no need of reward.
Having no aim or ambition,
It is the perfect host,
Whose warm presence is felt,
Celebrating us and not itself.

35. Creativity

Creativity is a sign of life.
Responding to it,
One is in a friendly place,
And will gladly wait.
Not tasting like food,
Yet one is nourished,
Not seen or heard,
Yet one s senses are open,
Going on forever,
Endlessly good.

36. Like Fish Out Of Water

Only those who are strong,
Can grow weak.
Only those who are a success,
Can be a failure.
Only those who need protection,
Can feel unprotected.
Only those who have been consequential,
Can feel belittled.
Those who are drawn to the outer,
Are like fish out of water.
Yet a person, who remains inner,
Flows with the water,
And following the nature of things,
Knows that like a fish,
They are best within their own depth.

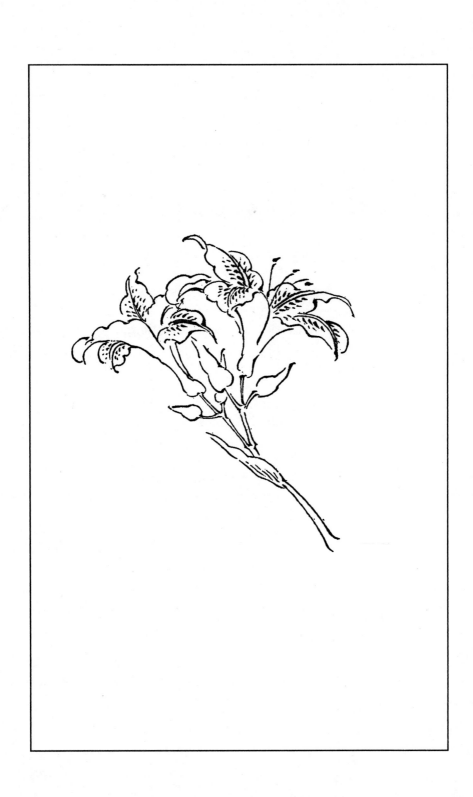

37. Non-Action

Doing nothing,
Allows all things to be done,
Action that arises out of being,
Appears as non-action,
Action that arises out of doing,
Appears as striving.
Those that know this,
Live transformed lives,
Listening to natural rhythms,
Allowing their strengths
To develop of their own accord.
Living in harmony,
They have no desire,
And without desire
They are content.

38. Beyond The Flower

A person, following their true path,
Is naturally creative,
Seemingly doing nothing,
They leave nothing undone.
A person, who has lost their way,
Tries to be creative, is always doing,
Yet gets nothing done.
One who is on their path,
Is not concerned with profits,
And does not need to pretend.
They are not concerned with power,
And do not need to convince.
When people lose their way,
They may listen to false prophets,
Who teach flowery methods,
Proclaiming the right way;
First goodness,
And when goodness is lost,
Morality,
And when morality is lost,
Ritual,
And when ritual is lost,
Authority.
While a person intent on living their life,
Goes beyond the flower to the fruit,
And dwelling in their own reality,
They know their yes,
And seek their best.

39. Listening To Stone Growing

Those who are in harmony with life,
Experience the strength of wholeness,
The heavens appear clear,
The earth is firm
Minds are free,
And everything flourishes.
When the wholeness of life is forgotten,
The heavens appear cloudy,
The earth infirm,
Minds are enslaved,
And everything decays.
Would you rather hear,
The tinkle of jade pendants,
Or listen,
To stone growing in a cliff.

40. Nothingness

From nothingness,
All things are created,
Arising from not being,
Being is born.
Once born,
All things open to life,
All life,
Yields to nothingness.

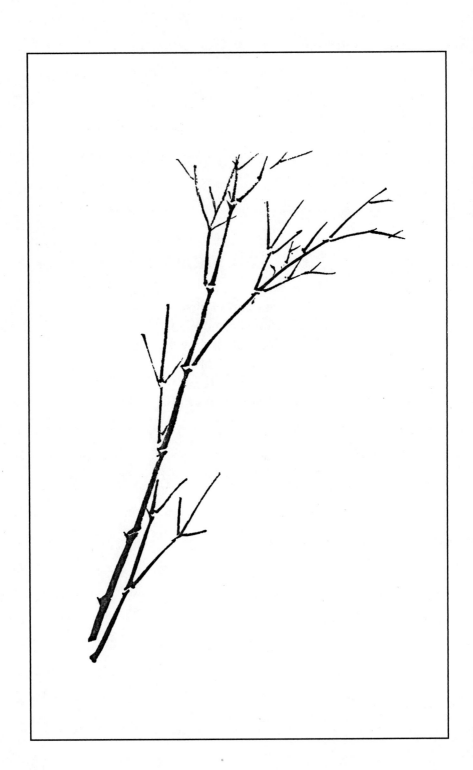

41. Listening

Some, when told to listen to themselves,
Immediately begin to hear,
Most, when told to follow their own way,
Travel only for awhile,
The foolish, may laugh and scorn.
The path often seems dark, long and winding,
Yet those who go straight around the circle,
Comprehend the whole.
Feeling beyond touch that which is hidden,
Hearing beyond sound the highest of notes,
Seeing beyond shapes the greatest of forms,
They are nourished and complete.

42. The Highs And Lows

Heaven - Earth - People,
Three elements of things,
Giving birth to all.
Encompassed by heaven,
Sustained by earth,
People give birth.
Embracing our aloneness,
We are nurtured,
By the whole universe.
Cool night, warm day,
Lightness, darkness,
The living and the dead.
Aware of the balance of happenings,
People living fully do not overreach,
Nor assert their might.
Accepting the highs and lows,
They live in wisdom s light.

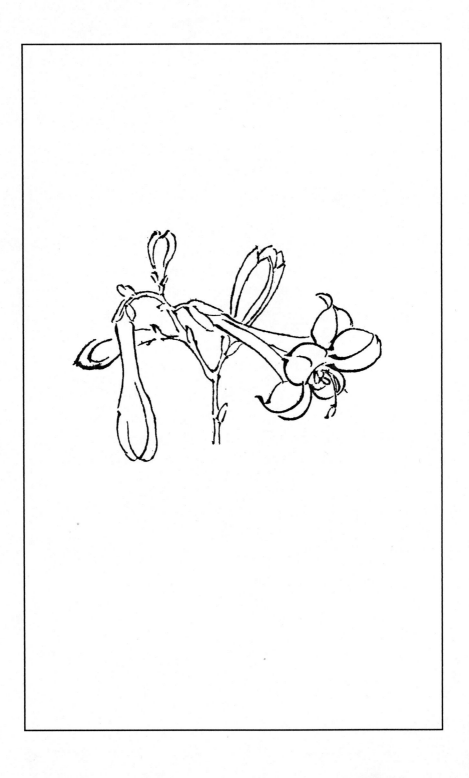

43. Shaping Stone

Soft yielding water
Shapes the hardest of stone.
Without asserting itself,
Water flows where others can t go.
To yield, to act without striving,
Is wisdom s way.
So too flowing with life,
Grinds the hardest of problems away.

44. The Richness Within

Which matters most,
Fame or self?
Which is most valuable,
Wealth or self?
Fame, wealth or self,
Which would be most missed?
Those who work for fame,
And those who work for wealth,
May lose themselves.
While those who work,
To do what they do best,
Continually grow themselves,
Finding richness within.

45. Incomplete Perfection

Great perfection,
Is always incomplete.
Great fullness,
Often appears empty.
The straightest of lines,
Seems curved.
The wisest of people,
Often act like children.
Since the truth,
Often appears opposite,
Suspend judgment.
Step out of the way,
Keep to what is,
And you will find your way.

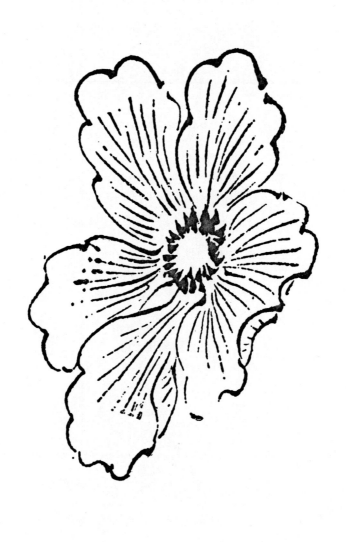

46. Forever Free

When you are in harmony,
With yourself,
You have all that you need.
When you are filled with desire,
Owning, wanting, taking,
You can lose the way.
Cursed with discontentment,
You may become warlike,
With yourself and others.
One who maintains contentment,
Knows the bliss of peace,
And is forever free.

47. Arrive Without Traveling

Without going outside,
Or gazing from a window,
One may see the light.
The further the traveler goes,
The less they may see,
And the less they may know.
Travel in your heart for guidance,
So you know which turns are wise.
Remaining at the core of your being,
You arrive without traveling,
See without looking,
Do without striving,

48. Needing Less And Less

Anxious to learn about life,
A person acquires more knowledge.
Content to be in life,
A person learns they need less and less.
Growing more and more,
Yet having less to do,
And less to keep in mind,
Their life takes its natural course,
And they and life are one.

49. Trust

A person whose heart is open,
Sees goodness and kindness in others,
Not being swayed by appearances,
They trust on a deeper level,
Seeing connections where others see none.
Appearing detached and humble,
Others look to them as to a parent,
And, yet, their heart remains like a child s.

50. Embracing Life And Death

They say that three in ten,
Are followers of life,
Three in ten are followers of death,
And three in ten value life,
Yet drift toward death.
The one leftover,
Lives fully in the moment,
Not being a follower of death,
Yet knowing that they will die,
They hold onto nothing,
Have no illusions
And embrace life and death as one.

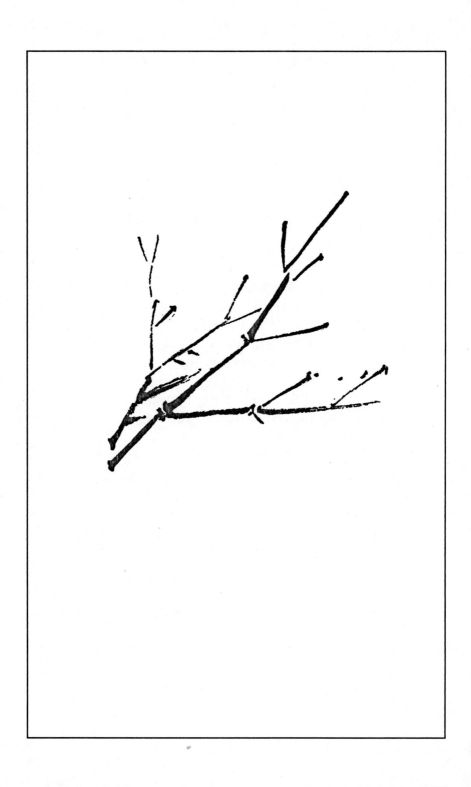

51. Free From Control

Our spirit is an expression,
Of our being,
Given freely to us,
It is ours to nourish,
In its many forms.
Best left to its own way,
Free from claim or control,
Its issue is spontaneously born.

52. Touching Eternity

Be fond of your creative manifestations,
Yet hold the core, the source dear.
The manifestations easily lead to judgments,
And may wrap you in desire,
Keeping your heart in the mire.
Focusing on the core, opens the heart,
Allows one to transcend time,
And touch eternity.

53. Real Wealth

The highway of inner learning,
Is broad and fit,
Yet people often follow side roads,
To find wealth, riches and power.
These fires of desire,
Are never satisfied,
For the more you have,
The more you think you need.
Yet the broad highway of being,
Offers the peace of inner strength,
The knowledge of connectedness to all,
And the real wealth of knowing,
You have enough.

54. Acknowledging Talents

Acknowledge your talents,
For they are a firm foundation,
On which to grow.
Embrace your strengths,
For they are a treasure,
Which none can steal.
Practicing what you love,
Will make you real,
Cultivating it in others,
Will help them grow,
Celebrating it in your community,
Will produce joy,
Supporting it in the nation,
Will make strong bonds.
How do you know this is so?
Look within and you will know.

55. In The Light

Whoever lives in harmony with themselves,
Will be in harmony,
With the forces of the world,
Stings will not poison them,
Attacks will not destroy them,
And predators will not conquer them.
Like a newborn child,
They are strong yet soft,
And their grasp is firm,
They may cry all day,
Yet their voice is clear and strong.
In wholeness,
They have no need of union with a mate,
Their personhood is strong.
That which they express,
Is done so without strain,
Without rush or desire,
For in perfect balance with life,
Their spirit is always in the light.

56. Unentangled

Those that know the most, do not speak,
Those who speak the most, do not know.
Those who live in harmony,
Do not waggle their tongues,
But rather curb their senses.
Remaining unentangled,
Without concern for profit or loss,
They are able to continually let go,
And so are continually filled up.

57. Without Interference

A country is governed by laws,
A battle won by strategy,
While our spirit is best nurtured,
By nothing at all.
Controlling it by rules,
Will leave you impoverished,
Forcing it, will leave you insecure,
Making it into work,
Will leave you in pain.
Our inner spirit, like people,
Does best when left alone,
Without interference,
Without demands or impositions,
It seeks to fulfill itself,
And enriches us all.

58. Appearances

When one trusts themselves,
They do not attempt to say,
That this is so or that is no.
Living a creative life they know that,
Often what appears to be so,
Contains the seeds of it s opposite.
Not knowing which way the circle turns,
They do not know what is the cause,
And what is the result,
Letting go of their own will,
They are in harmony with the will of the way,
And their life provides,
Light without glare,
Strength without aggression,
And guidance without teaching.

59. Bonded With Life

A person who is sparked
By their own spirit,
Joins the one source,
Doubling theirs, of course.
So bonded with life
They can only go right,
And like a good parent,
Give love and light.

60. Talents Growing

Handle your life gently,
As if frying a small fish.
By letting it simmer,
No demons will arise to taunt you,
No ghosts to suppress you.
With nothing to oppose,
The ghosts will lie fallow,
Nurturing the ground,
From which your talents,
Will naturally grow.

61. Like The Sea

A person who is living well,
Is like the sea,
Drawn to it,
All rivers flow.
Yet the larger it grows,
The humbler it is,
Still needing the small,
It lies low.

62. Curiosity

Life is for all,
A good person s wealth,
A bad person s survival.
Beyond the bounds of good or bad,
Curiosity is for all,
For through it,
You may find what you seek.
All of this is free,
And cannot be bought,
By clever words or deeds.

63. Accomplish Without Struggle

A person living on purpose,
Learns to accomplish,
Without struggle,
Keeping things small and manageable,
Allows them to achieve wonderful things.
The greatest problems in the world,
Are often made large,
By those reaching for greatness.
A person unconcerned about greatness,
Sees no problems as too big,
No difficulties as too small.
Acting naturally within the moment,
They embrace each facet,
Learn to love each foe,
And unencumbered will have it all.

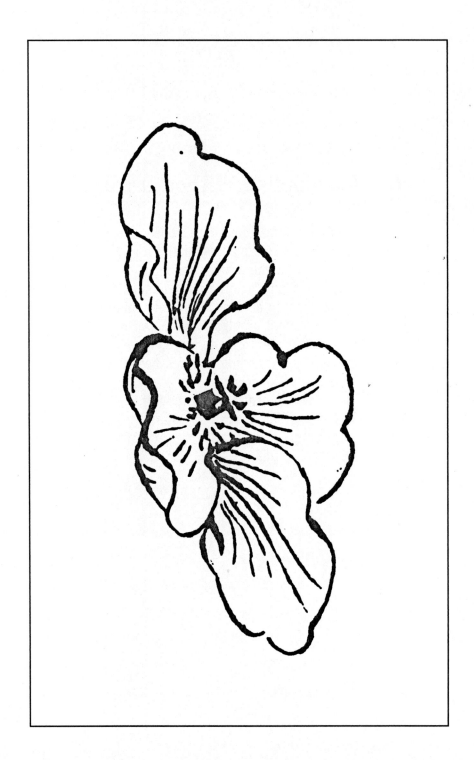

64. Paying Attention

Pay attention to what is,
In order to prevent what is not,
A cut needs cleaning,
A relationship needs tending,
A hurt needs caring.
Pay attention to what is,
In order to grow what is not,
A joy needs sharing,
An idea needs nurturing,
A vision needs expressing.
The greatest of pine trees,
Is deeply rooted,
Yet grows easily,
From the smallest of seeds.

65. Less Knowledge

Those who follow their own way,
Do not attempt to teach others
Through knowledge.
A wise teacher does not preach,
For they know that the more you know,
The less you may understand,
And the more you understand,
The less you may need to know.

66. Like The Ocean

By lying low, open and clear,
The river accepts all streams,
The ocean accepts all rivers.
Life, like an ocean,
Is nourished by many streams;
The flow of intuition,
The bubbling of imagination,
The swirling of ideas,
The splashing of playfulness.
Like the ocean,
It accepts all streams,
Never judging,
Never obstructing their way.
If leadership is needed,
Be like the ocean,
Remaining low, humble,
Accepting all.
Like all waters,
Each will find their own level,
And grow to fulfill their potential.

67. Three Gifts That Guide

Some say that those who live a life
Based on their uniqueness are too simple,
For they may not be involved in a worldly way,
Their aims too impractical, too full of play.
Alive with three treasures they hold dear,
They continue to follow their own way;
Compassion towards themselves,
And others,
Makes them unafraid,
Fairness and simplicity,
Endows them with a generous spirit,
And not seeking to rise to the top,
Their humility sets them free.
These three gifts,
Compassion, simplicity and humility,
Guide them in a gentle way,
And guard them from a living death.

68. Excellence

Those who excel,
Do not live life as if in a battle.
Like a good general,
Who is one with their enemy,
They are not violent.
Like a good fighter,
Who uses their opponent s strength,
They are not angry.
Like a good victor,
Who is compassionate
With their conquests,
They are not vengeful.
And like a good leader,
Who sees the worth in all,
They are not arrogant.
They live life as if playing,
And are able to include it all.

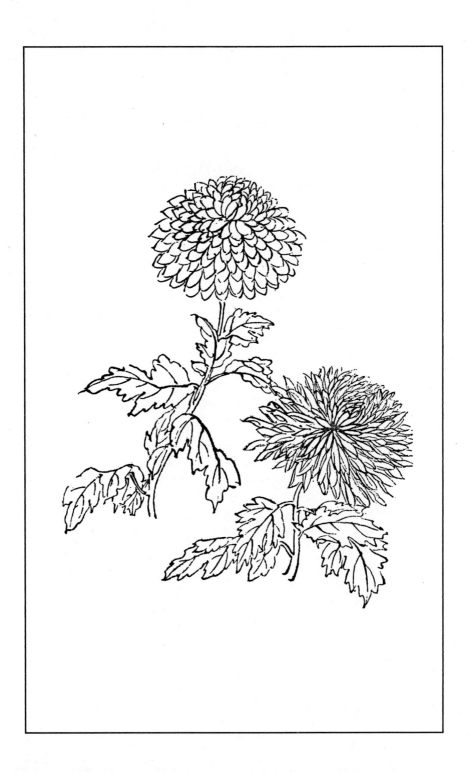

69. Handling Opposition

When faced with opposition,
Be a master strategist,
Do not invite a fight,
Act like a guest.
Accepting, yet not advancing,
Yielding, yet not withdrawing,
Learning, yet not attacking,
Respect and value your foe.
Be one with your opposition,
So there is no battle to fight.

70. Following Strengths

Following one s strengths is easy,
To put into practice
And to understand,
For it is the natural way.
Yet being so easy and free,
Few practice or understand it.
The few who do follow this way,
May dress in simple clothes,
Yet hold a treasure of jewels
Within their hearts,
And their lives display,
The enormous wealth,
Of following their own way.

71. Seeking The Light

A seeker of inner truth knows,
That they do not know,
And uses their not knowing,
To search for the light.
A fearful, rigid person,
Does not know,
That they do not know,
And not seeking the light,
Stays in darkness.

72. Living Fully

When people lose their sense of wonder,
Darkness reigns,
Mediocrity rules,
Laws and rituals take over,
Intruding into minds and hearts,
Growing conformity,
Deadening lives.
Those that live their lives fully,
Know themselves with no need of show,
Respect themselves with no need of praise,
And having no need of oppression,
Or interference,
They prefer their within to that without.

73. Demands No Obedience

Some are better,
At mastering the things of the world,
While some are better,
At mastering things within.
Being true to their own talents,
Each is unafraid,
And being unafraid,
May live in a creative way.
Each contain traits of the other,
Some good, some bad,
Whose to judge the spirit s way,
Since the universe gives no advice,
And demands no obedience,
Yet is there, encouraging all.

74. Fear

It is logical that if people,
Are afraid to die,
They will risk little,
And do no wrong ,
If threatened with death.
Yet death belongs to nature,
And is not ours to say.
Those who judge,
And play executioner,
With themselves or others,
Will not be open to their choices,
And may kill their inner voice,
So listen to your heart,
Let go of control,
And be who you are.

75. Demands

Do not demand too much,
Of your creativity,
For if taxed too heavily,
It will not thrive.
Rules and laws only interfere
Causing it to rebel.
It s spirit is alive and well,
And if left alone,
It will be expressed,
For it does not treat death lightly,
And loves to be heard.

76. Tender And Yielding

Born into life tender,
Pliant and soft,
All things enter death hard,
Rigid and cold.
So it is that those closer to life,
Are gentle and yielding,
While those closer to death,
Are stiff and unyielding.
Rock can only crumble,
Wind can change,
Tender and yielding is life s way.

77. A Master Archer

A person of true balance,
Acts like a master archer,
Who in bending the bow,
Lowers the top and raises the low,
Taking from what is too much
Adding to what is not.
Those who want power and control,
Being out of balance,
Take from those with too little
To benefit those with too much.
One s spirit responds like a bow,
Wanting to stay in balance,
It follows the natural way,
Yielding without force,
Aimed from the heart it finds it s way.

78. Persistence

There is nothing,
So soft and yielding,
As water,
Yet it can shape,
The hardest of stones.
When faced,
With an obstacle,
Put this into practice,
Be not hard and resist,
But yield and persist.

79. Flow

When a project does not work out,
A person who stays attuned to their purpose,
Does not blame, does not pout.
Not expecting,
Not demanding,
They continue to put in their full,
Allowing non-attachment,
Detaching from results,
They are able to let go,
And flow with the journey.

80. Simplicity

A person who feels empty,
Does not know they have enough,
Is driven by greed,
And rushes about.
A person who is content,
Has no need to save time,
And fully savors each moment.
Although they may have access,
To fancy clothes and expensive lodgings,
They follow the simple way,
Choosing freedom over things,
Energy becomes more important than matter,
And being at home within themselves,
They do each day their own way.

81. Play

Boastful words are used,
By those who have not yet found their way.
Boastful words are not needed,
By those who are following their spirit s way.
With no need to argue or prove their point,
They enjoy their presence in the world.
With no need to act,
Nor to hold back,
They trust themselves,
For life is spontaneous play.

About the Authors

Judith Morgan and Andre de Zanger are the co-directors of the Creativity Institute in New York City. As international consultants in the field of creativity, they lead workshops and seminars for corporations around the world.

Morgan and de Zanger are the authors of *Verti-Think*: *Techniques for Generating New Ideas*, *Zingers*: *Creativity Word Games*, *The Tao of Creativity*, *Creativity Therapy* and *Instant Selling: Tools for Creative Selling*. They have also developed a computer software program which contains techniques to stimulate creativity and to solve problems in innovative ways.